Follow Me

Themes from the Bible retold for children
by

A. J. McCallen

Illustrations by Ferelith Eccles Williams

COLLINS

🔲 ABRAHAM TRUSTED GOD

Abraham trusted God and he believed what God told him,
for he knew that God would not let him down.

The Reading comes from the Book of Beginnings.

God told Abraham that he would be famous.
He promised to look after Abraham's family,
and he said he would give them somewhere to live.

But Abraham lived in a tent,
and wandered around the desert with his sheep,
and he didn't even have any children.

One night Abraham was standing outside his tent,
looking up at the stars,
and he wondered how many stars there were.
He couldn't even begin to count them all!
Then God told him,
'You will have as many children as there are stars!'
And Abraham believed what God said.
Then he fell asleep
and dreamed that God came to him
like a great fire that burned in the dark!
And God said,
'I promise you, I will be your friend.'

2

This poem was written by a man like Abraham who knew he could trust God all the time. It comes from the Book of Praise.

Blessed be God!

He listens to me,
he hears me when I pray for help.
Blessed be God!

I trust the Lord
for he is strong.
Blessed be God!

I thank the Lord
for he takes care of me.
Blessed be God!

Jesus reminds us that Abraham trusted God and believed in him.

The Reading comes from the Gospel of Saint John.

One day, Jesus was talking to some people
who were angry with him.

They said,
'We don't believe what *your* Father says,
we only believe what Abraham has told us.
Abraham is our "Father",
and we don't want to know anything about *your* Father!'

But Jesus replied,
'If you were really children of Abraham,
you would believe in my Father
just as Abraham himself did!
And you wouldn't want to kill me
just because I have told you what my Father has said.
Abraham would never have done that!'

⊠ MOSES WAS NEARLY KILLED!

Moses was nearly drowned when he was a little baby. But God took extra special care of him because he wanted Moses to be the leader of his People when he grew up.

The Reading comes from the Book of Moses.

A long time ago
a man became King in Egypt
who hated the Jews,
because there were so many of them.
So he decided
to have all the Jewish baby boys drowned!

One day a Jewish baby was born
and his mother thought he was so beautiful
that she hid him away and kept him alive.
But in the end he became too big to hide,
and she had to find a way to get rid of him safely.
So she got a basket and painted it with tar
to keep out the water,
and she put her baby in the basket
and left the basket floating in the river.
But she told her daughter
to keep watching it
to see what happened to him.

A Princess came down to the river to have a swim,
and one of her servants saw the basket
as she walked along the riverside.
'Pull it out!' said the Princess,
so the servant did
and the Princess felt so sorry for the baby
she decided to keep him.

Just then the baby's sister came along and said,
'Shall I find someone to look after the baby for you?'
and the Princess said 'Yes.'

4

So the little girl went to get her own mother,
and then the Princess *paid* the woman
to look after *her own* baby!
But when the baby grew up,
the Princess made him just like her own son
and called him Moses.

*Jesus was nearly killed when he was a baby – just like Moses! But God
the Father did not want him to die so soon and took good care of him, so
Jesus escaped.*

The Reading comes from the Gospel of Saint Matthew.

Soon after Jesus was born,
Joseph was told that King Herod was looking for the child
and wanted to kill him!

Some Wise Men had come to King Herod
and told him that a new king called Jesus
was going to be born in Bethlehem.
They had promised to come back again
when they found him
and tell King Herod where he was,
but then they didn't come back at all,
and the King was furious!
So he murdered *all* the little baby boys in Bethlehem!

But Joseph escaped into Egypt with Jesus and his mother.

⊞ SAMUEL: THE BOY WHO LISTENED TO GOD

This is the story of Samuel, the boy who heard the voice of God.
The Reading comes from the Story of the Kings.

A long, long time ago,
there was a priest called Eli.
He was very old and was going blind.
But a young boy, called Samuel, looked after him.

One night, while Samuel was in bed,
he heard someone calling his name,
'Samuel! Samuel!'
So he got up and went to Eli and said,
'Here I am, what do you want?'
But Eli said,
'*I* didn't call you!
Go back to bed.'
So Samuel went and lay down again.

But it happened once more,
and Samuel went back to Eli,
and again Eli told him to go back to bed!

But when it happened a third time,
Eli said,
'Next time you must say,
"Yes, Lord, I'm listening." '

And it did happen again,
for God came and stood beside Samuel
and called his name,
and Samuel said,
'Yes, Lord, I'm listening.'
And then God spoke to Samuel,
and told him what he was going to do.

After that God was always very close to Samuel
and when the boy grew up,
he always listened to what God told him.

6

We talk to God in our prayers and then he is very close to us as well.

The Reading comes from the Gospel of Saint Matthew.

One day Jesus said,
'When you say your prayers,
don't worry so much about the things you want,
remember that you have a Father in Heaven
who knows all about the things you need.

'When *you* say your prayers,
promise him to try and do what he wants,
and he will give you everything you need as well!'

🔢 DAVID: THE BOY WHO LOOKED AFTER THE SHEEP

This is the story of a boy called David who was very close to God.
The Reading comes from the Book of Samuel.

A long, long time ago there was a man called Samuel.

One day God told Samuel to go and choose someone
to be the new king.
God said,
'I want you to find a new king for me.
I don't mind what he looks like!
He doesn't have to be tall and handsome!
Some people only think a man is good if he *looks* good,
but I can see how good a man really is!'

Samuel went to Bethlehem
to the house of a man called Jesse,
and he looked at the seven sons of Jesse one by one.
But he knew God did not want any of these!

So he said,
'Have you any more children?'
'Yes,' said Jesse,
'you haven't seen my youngest boy yet,
but he's out, looking after the sheep.'
'Bring him here,' said Samuel,
and Jesse brought in David.

David was a good-looking boy
with red cheeks and bright eyes,
and Samuel knew at once that *he* was the right person!

So he blessed David
and poured oil on his head
(to show that God was going to make him strong and good).
And from then on
God was always very close to the boy.

Jesus prays that God may be close to all of us, then we will know that he loves us.

The Reading comes from the Gospel of Saint John.

Just before he died,
Jesus said this prayer to his Father in heaven.

'Father, keep my friends safe!
May you be as close to them
  as you are close to me.
And may they be happy
  and free from all harm!'

✠ DAVID AND GOLIATH

This is the story of how David killed Goliath, even though David was only a little boy and Goliath was a big strong man.
The Reading comes from the Book of Samuel.

A long, long time ago there was a boy called David,
who lived with his seven brothers in Bethlehem.
His three eldest brothers were soldiers,
and one day their father sent David
to the camp where all the soldiers lived
to take some bread and cheese to his brothers.

David got up early that morning
and asked someone else to look after his sheep for him,
then he set off for the camp.

9

When he got there,
the soldiers were getting ready to start fighting,
so David left his bag
    with the man who looked after the luggage,
and went to see his brothers as quickly as he could.
While he was talking to them,
Goliath, the best soldier in the enemy army, came along
and said he would fight anyone who thought they could beat him.
But everyone ran away
because they were all afraid of him.

So David said,
'What will you give me if I kill him?'
But his brothers said,
'No, you can't!
Go away, go home!
What are you doing here anyway?
Who is looking after your sheep?
You've just come here for the fun of it
    to see the fighting.'

King Saul heard what David had said
and sent for him.
'You can't go and fight Goliath,' said King Saul.
'You're only a little boy,
and he's a big tall man!'
But David said,
'Oh yes I can!
I have killed a lion and a bear before now
    when they attacked my sheep,
so I can easily kill Goliath!'

So the King said,
'Well, you can always have a go.
May God help you.
You can use my breast plate and my helmet,
and you can take my big sword with you as well.'
But David said,
'I couldn't even walk with all those on,
I'm not used to wearing them!

All I want is my stick and my sling
and five smooth pebbles from the river.'

When little David came out with his sling,
Goliath just laughed at him.
But David said,
'Don't laugh! You think you are strong
    because you have a sword and a spear,
but I have God to help me
    and he is much stronger than you are!'
Then he put a stone in his sling,
swung it round and round,
and let it go,
and the stone flew straight towards Goliath
and hit him on the forehead and killed him!

Then all the enemy soldiers ran away
when they saw their best soldier had been killed!

*David was obviously very brave. In this reading Jesus tells us that we must
be brave as well.*

The Reading comes from the Gospel of Saint Luke.

Jesus spent the last few days of his life in Jerusalem,
and each day he went to the Temple to teach the people
– this is what he said to them:

'Keep praying that you will be brave,
pray that you will keep going
and then you won't let me down!'

Lots of people used to come to the Temple each morning
    just to hear Jesus,
and he stayed there all day long speaking to them.
Then in the evening
Jesus would go out to the Olive Hill near Jerusalem
    to pray during the night.

⊠ DAVID AND JONATHAN

David and Jonathan were the best of friends. They knew they could trust each other and they knew they would never let each other down.

The Reading comes from the Story of Samuel.

A long time ago there was a king called Saul,
who became very unhappy with himself,
   though he didn't know why.
One day he said to his soldiers,
'Find me a man who can play the harp really well,
and bring him to me
so that he can play for me and cheer me up.'
One of his soldiers said,
'I have seen David, the son of Jesse, playing the harp,
and he plays very well indeed.
He's also a brave fighter and very sensible.'

So King Saul sent for David,
and when he came,
the King asked him to stay with him.
Whenever the King felt upset and miserable,
David used to play his harp
and the King would listen.
Then he would feel much better again.
King Saul thought David was wonderful.

The King had a son called Jonathan,
and Jonathan became David's friend.
In fact they became such good friends
that one day Jonathan gave David his cloak and his belt
   and his sword and bow as well,
and they promised to be friends for ever.

Everyone liked David
for he was such a good fighter.

But then King Saul began to get jealous of him,
and one day, when the King was feeling upset and miserable,
he said to Jonathan,
'I am going to kill David!'

So Jonathan went out to his friend and said,
'My father wants to kill you,
so you must go and hide in the fields,
until I find out what's wrong,
then I'll come and let you know.'

Next morning, Jonathan went back to his father and said,
'Please don't hurt David.
He's done nothing wrong to you.
He has done everything possible to help you.'
In the end he made his father agree with him,
and King Saul said,
'I promise God
I will not hurt your friend.'
So Jonathan went to David
and told him everything that had happened,
and he brought David back to live with the King again.

It's good to have friends, especially when we know they will not let us down. Jesus liked his friends just as we do, and he liked to be together with them, as all friends do.

The Reading comes from the Gospel of Saint Mark.

Jesus went round all the villages near Nazareth
and he told everyone the 'Good News from God'.
Then he called 'the Twelve' together
and sent them out in twos
so that they could go and do the same as him.

When they came back,
they wanted to tell Jesus
about all the things they had said
and everything they had done.
So Jesus said,
'You haven't even had time for anything to eat.
Let's go away to a quiet place
by ourselves,
and have a rest.'

So they did,
and they all went off to a quiet place
where they could be by themselves.

✠ JOHN THE BAPTIST

John the Baptist said – 'Get ready for God!' So did Isaiah.
The Reading comes from the Book of a Wise Man called Isaiah.

A long, long time ago, Isaiah said,

Can you hear the voice of God?
Listen to what he is saying.

'Make a straight road for him to walk along.
Fill in the valleys,
and flatten the hills.'

Then you will see God.
Everyone will see him,
for God has said so himself!

✠

Except for Jesus himself, there never was anyone greater than John the
Baptist!

The Reading comes from the Gospel of Saint Matthew.

John the Baptist lived down by the River Jordan.
He didn't wear expensive clothes,
and he didn't eat very much,
but lots of people came to see him.

He used to say,
'Stop doing wrong,
God is going to send you a King.'

Then everyone would tell God they were sorry
for doing wrong,
and John would pour water over them in the river,
(and make them clean).

⊞ MARY AND ELIZABETH

This is the story of how Mary went to look after Elizabeth while Elizabeth was having a baby.

The Reading comes from the Gospel of Saint Luke.

One day, Mary heard
that her cousin, Elizabeth, was going to have a baby.

So she went as quickly as she could
into the hills to the town where Elizabeth lived.

Mary went into Elizabeth's house
and said 'Hello, how are you?'
And Elizabeth replied,
'I am proud
that you have come to visit me,
because the Lord has given you
a special blessing!
He has given you a special child!'

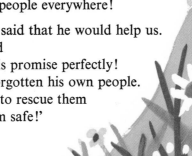

Then Mary said,
'I praise the Lord for he is good.
He makes me glad!
I am young and I am poor,
and yet he comes and chooses me!
And from now on,
everyone will say that he has blessed me.

'The Lord is strong, the Lord is generous,
stretching out his hand to help the sick,
feeding hungry people with good food,
looking after people everywhere!

'Long ago he said that he would help us.
Now the Lord
      has kept his promise perfectly!
He has not forgotten his own people.
He has come to rescue them
and keep them safe!'

16

✠

Jesus said 'If you want to be like my mother, you must do what God the Father wants.'

The Reading comes from the Gospel of Saint Mark.

One day Jesus went home
and so many people came to see him
and he was so busy
that he didn't even have time to eat anything.

When his family heard about this
they said he was mad,
and they came along to help him.
But there were so many people outside the house
they couldn't even get anywhere near him.
So they sent him a message, saying,
'Your mother and the rèst of your family
 are outside
and they want to see you.'

Inside the house
everyone was sitting round Jesus in a circle,
and he looked round at them all and said,
'You will all be my brothers and my sisters
and my mother as well,
if you do what God wants you to do.'

✥ MARY KNOWS HOW TO PRAY

When almost everyone else had run away Mary stood by the cross near her Son. At least she didn't let him down.

The Reading comes from the Gospel of Saint John.

When Jesus was on the cross,
his mother stood beside him,
and her sister was there as well,
and Mary of Magdala.

Jesus looked at his mother,
and he looked at John, his best friend,
who was standing beside her,
and he said,
'Mother,
John will take care of you
   as if he was your own son.'
Then he said to John,
'I know she will be like a mother to you.'

And when Jesus had died,
John took Mary home
   to stay with him.

While the followers of Jesus were waiting for the Holy Spirit to come and tell them what to do, they spent most of their time praying together, and Mary was there to pray with them.

The Reading comes from the Story of the Apostles.

After the Ascension,
the friends of Jesus went back to the city,
and stayed in the room where they lived.

All the friends of Jesus were there,
Peter, John, James and Andrew,
Philip, Thomas and Bartholomew,
and Matthew, James, Simon and Jude.

And the women who were friends of Jesus
were there as well,
– and his mother, Mary.

And they spent their time together, praying.

THE FRIENDS OF JESUS STAY WITH HIM

Even when the other people said they wouldn't follow Jesus, 'The Twelve' did not let him down.

The Reading comes from the Gospel of Saint John.

One day a lot of the friends of Jesus said,
'We don't like the things he tells us.
No one can believe *him*!'

Jesus heard them complaining and said,
'Why are you upset?'

But after that,
a lot of them left him,
and wouldn't follow him.

Then Jesus turned to 'The Twelve' and said,
'What about you?
Will you leave me as well?'

But Peter said,
'Who else could we go to?
You can tell us how to live,
and we believe what you tell us.'

We must try to follow Jesus like 'The Twelve', even if people try to put us off.
The Reading comes from one of the Letters of Saint Paul.

Dear Friends,

I can see God our Father loves you.
He has picked you out in a special way.

When I told you about Jesus,
it really made a difference to you
and you began to try and live like Jesus,
even though some people tried to put you off!

20

✠ SAINT PETER TELLS A LIE

Do not tell lies about anyone!

The Reading comes from one of the Letters of Saint Paul.

Dear Titus,
Don't forget that we have all been silly sometimes,
and we have all done wrong ourselves.
There was a time
when we were horrible to people
and they didn't like us
because we were always doing wrong.

But then Jesus came to us
and showed us how to be kind.

So don't tell any more lies about people
and be friendly and polite to everyone.

✠

*No one would have thought that Saint Peter would tell a lie about Jesus,
and yet he did! But then he was very sorry for it and Jesus forgave him.*

The Reading comes from the Gospel of Saint Matthew.

When Jesus was arrested,
he was taken away to the Palace to be questioned.
So Peter followed him
    to see what was going to happen,
and he sat down in the courtyard outside the Palace
    and waited.

A servant girl came up to him and said,
'You were with Jesus of Galilee, weren't you?'
But he denied it in front of everyone and said,
'I don't know what you are talking about!'
Then he walked away
and stood near the gate.

Another servant girl saw him there
and she said to all the people,
'This man was with Jesus of Nazareth!'
Peter denied it again and said,
'By God, I do not know the man!'

A little later someone else came up and said,
'You are one of them, I know,
I can tell by the way you speak.'
Then Peter began to curse and swear,
'I tell you, I don't know him.'

Just then the cock crew
    and Peter suddenly remembered that Jesus had said:
'Peter, you will let me down in the morning!'
And when he thought of what he had just done,
    he went outside and began to cry
    for he was ashamed of himself.

✙ SAINT MATTHEW, THE TAX MAN

God is always ready to forgive us.

The Reading comes from the Book of a Wise Man called Joel.

God says this –

Come back to me
    and be sorry.
Turn back to me,
    for I am gentle.

I am slow to lose my temper
and very quick to forgive you
    if you have done wrong.

✙

This is the story of Matthew, the Tax Man.

The Reading comes from the Gospel of Saint Matthew.

One day Jesus met a man called Matthew
who was a tax collector.
He was sitting in his house working
when Jesus came,
but Jesus said,
'Follow me!'
and Matthew got up at once
    and followed him.

Then he took Jesus for a meal
and he invited a lot of his old friends as well.
Some of the Teachers saw this and they said,
'Matthew's old friends are bad people!
Why does Jesus go and eat with *them*?'

But Jesus heard them saying this and said,
'I have come to *help* bad people, that's why.
I can't help the people who think they're all right!'

✠ A RICH MAN CALLED ZACHAEUS

When we do wrong, we turn away from God. But God wants us to come back to him and he will help us to do so – like the shepherd who even carries back the sheep on his shoulders.

The Reading comes from the Gospel of Saint Luke.

One day Jesus said,

'If you had a hundred sheep,
and you lost one of them,
wouldn't you go and look for that one lost sheep
even if you had to leave all the others
   on the hillside by themselves?

'And when you found it again,
wouldn't you be happy
as you carried it home on your shoulders?
You would be so happy,
you would tell everyone else about it
   so that they could share your happiness.

'In the same way,
even if only one man has run away from God,
God will still be very happy
to welcome him back home.'

God is very happy to see anyone come back to him. But if we have done wrong by stealing, he would like us to give back what we have taken before we come and tell him we are sorry.

The Reading comes from the Gospel of Saint Luke.

One day, Jesus went to Jericho.

Now a man lived there called Zachaeus,
and he was very rich,
because he collected money for the Romans.

This man was very keen to see what Jesus looked like,
but he was only little,
and he couldn't see anything with all the people there.

So he ran on in front,
and climbed up a sycamore tree
just to see Jesus when he went past.
But Jesus saw him up the tree and said,
'Come down, I want to stay in your house today.'
So Zachaeus climbed down as quickly as he could,
and took him home.

Everyone else complained and said,
'He's a bad man,
Jesus shouldn't have gone there.'
But Zachaeus said,
'Look Jesus,
I'm going to give half of everything I've got to the poor!
And if I've cheated anyone,
I'll give him back four times as much as I took!'

✪ THE SOLDIER WHO DID AS HE WAS TOLD

*It's no good just saying you will do something, to keep people happy,
if you are not really going to do it.*

The Reading comes from the Gospel of Saint Matthew.

One day Jesus said,
I'm going to tell you a story,
and I want to know what you think about it.

There was a man who had two sons.
He went to one of the sons and said,
'Will you go and do a job for me today?'
but the lad said,
'No, I won't!'
Then later on he felt sorry
and he went and did the job!

The Father went to the other boy
and said the same thing
This boy said,
'Yes, certainly!'
But then he didn't go at all!

Then Jesus said,
'Which boy did what his Father wanted?'
And everyone said the same,
'It was the first boy
   for he did the job in the end.'

⊞

This is the story of the Roman Soldier who was certain that Jesus could help his servant.

The Reading comes from the Gospel of Saint Luke.

There was once a Roman Soldier
and he had a servant who was ill and dying.
Now this servant was a very good servant,
so the Soldier sent some of his friends
to ask Jesus if he would come and help him.

When these friends came to Jesus, they said,
'This man has been very good to us.
He has even built our meeting house for us.'

So Jesus went along to the Soldier's house
and when he was nearly there,
the Soldier sent him another message, saying,
'Please don't let me trouble you!
I'm not good enough for you to come to me.
But if you just tell my servant to be better,
then I'm sure he will be all right again!
You see I know you can do this
because I am a soldier,
and *I* always do as I'm told.
I also expect everyone else to do the same!
If I say "Go!"
    then people go where I tell them.
If I say "Come here!"
    then they come to me.
If I say "Do that!"
    then they get on with it at once.'

When Jesus heard this, he was surprised
    and very pleased.
        'I haven't seen many people trust me like this,' he said.

    So he sent the messenger back to the Soldier
        and when they got back
            they found the servant was already better.

✠ THE MAN WHO CAME IN THROUGH THE ROOF

God is our Father and he can do anything!

The Reading comes from the Book of a Wise Man called Jeremiah.

God says,

Do not be afraid, my people,
for I will come and help you.

I hear that you are very ill!
No one can cure you,
no one can help you
and you cannot find a medicine
that will do you any good.

But I will make you healthy once more.
Yes I will make you better!

✠

Jesus is like God our Father, he can do anything! The man on the stretcher obviously believed this!

The Reading comes from the Gospel of Saint Mark.

When Jesus came back to Capernaum
the news got round that he was back
and so many people came to listen to him
they filled the house where he was,
and there wasn't even a space left in front of the door.

While Jesus was talking,
four men came with a man on a stretcher,
This man was paralysed and couldn't walk by himself,
and they wanted to bring him to Jesus.

30

There was no room for them to get in through the door.
So they made a hole in the roof
    just over the place where Jesus was standing,
and lowered the stretcher down in front of him.

It was obvious they believed that Jesus could help the man.
Jesus could see that clearly,
so he said,
'Stand up, my friend.
Pick up your stretcher and go home.'
And the man *got* up,
    and picked up his stretcher at once,
    and walked out of the house all by himself!

Everyone was astonished when they saw this,
and they said:

'How good God is!'

✣ THE GOOD THIEF

We should never be spiteful.
The Reading comes from one of the Letters of Saint Paul.

Dear Friends,

From now on there's going to be no more telling lies.
You are going to tell the truth instead.

If you get angry with someone,
I want you to try and become friends again
   as soon as you can on the same day.

Don't lose your temper.
Don't shout at each other.
Don't call each other names,
and don't be spiteful!

Remember you have received
the gift of the Holy Spirit.
Therefore be friends with each other,
and forgive each other quickly,
because God has been quick to forgive you.

☒

The bad thief was spiteful to Jesus, but the good thief became a saint!
The Reading comes from the Gospel of Saint Luke.

Jesus died on a cross,
at a place called the Hill of the Skull,
and two thieves were killed with him,
  one on either side.

There was a sign nailed to the cross of Jesus
and it said,
'This is the King of the Jews.'
So one of the thieves said,
'You're not much of a King, are you!'
But the other thief said,
'Don't say that!
He hasn't done anything wrong.'

Then he turned to Jesus and said,
'Don't forget me, will you?'

Jesus said,
'I promise you,
I will take you to heaven with me today!'

✠ THE BAPTISM OF SAINT PAUL

No one would have expected Saul to become a follower of Jesus. But strange things sometimes happen, and the greatest enemy of Jesus became his greatest friend.

The Reading comes from the Story of the Apostles.

A long time ago, there was a man called Saul,
and he hated the friends of Jesus so much
that he wanted to kill them all.
So he got permission to hunt them out
and put them in prison.

One day, he was riding on horse-back
to a city called Damascus,
and just as he came to the city walls,
he was thrown from his horse,
and saw a great flash of light.

Then he heard someone saying,
'Saul, Saul, why are you hurting me?'
'Who's that?' he said.
'I'm Jesus,' said the voice,
'and you're hurting *me*!'

Then Saul tried to get up,
but he couldn't see,
even with his eyes wide open.
Someone had to take his hand
and lead him into the city.

Jesus then sent a man called Ananias
to go and visit Saul.
Ananias didn't want to go
because he had heard all about this man
and he was afraid of him.
But God said he must go, so he did.

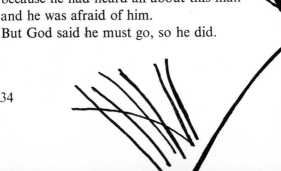

When Ananias found Saul,
he was saying his prayers
in a house in Straight Street.
So he went in and blessed him
with his hands outstretched over Saul.
'Brother Saul,' he said,
'Jesus has sent me to help you.
Receive the Holy Spirit.'
And at once Saul could see again,
    and he asked to be baptised immediately.

Jesus wants everyone to come to him,
then they will get to know and love his Father
and receive the Holy Spirit.

The Reading comes from the Gospel of Saint
Matthew.

Jesus said,

I want you to go everywhere
    and tell everyone what I have done.

Go and baptise them
    in the name of the Father
                and of the Son
                and of the Holy Spirit.

I have shown you how you should live,
now you must teach others to do the same.
I promise you
        I will always be near you to help you.

✥ 'THE HARD LIFE!'

Jesus tells us that he always had to work very hard.
The Reading comes from the Gospel of Saint Luke.

One day Jesus was walking from one village to another
and a man came up to him and said,
'Jesus, I will follow you wherever you go!'

Jesus was pleased to hear him saying this
but he said to the man,
'You have to be ready to work hard,
   if you are going to follow me, you know.
Even a fox can go down a hole in the ground
   to have a rest,
and the birds can go back to their nests.
But I haven't even got a house to sleep in!'

It's hard work following in the footsteps of Jesus, as Saint Paul discovered for himself.

The Reading comes from one of the Letters of Saint Paul.

Dear Friends,

These are some of the things that have happened to me
while I have been telling people about Jesus.
I have had to work very hard.

I've been sent to prison.
I've been beaten up
  (in fact I was nearly killed once!)
I've been shipwrecked
  (and once I was lost out at sea all night!)

I've always been on the move
and I've often been afraid
  that I was going to be attacked by bandits.
I've had to get across rivers
  when there's been no bridge to walk over.

I've often had to go on working
without going to bed all night.

Sometimes I've been so hungry and thirsty
  that I've nearly died!

Once I even had some soldiers chasing me
and I had to get away by hiding in a basket
  and my friends lowered me out of their window
    over the city walls
  so that I could escape and go free.

Nevertheless I can put up with all this,
because I am doing it all for the sake of Jesus.

✠ SAINT STEPHEN FORGAVE THE PEOPLE WHO KILLED HIM

We must always be ready to keep on forgiving people even if they do hurt us.

The Reading comes from the Gospel of Saint Luke.

One day Jesus said,

'If your friend does you wrong,
you can tell him off, if you like,
but if he says sorry,
　you must forgive him.
Even if he does wrong and upsets you
　seven times each day,
but then comes to you
　and says he is really sorry
you must keep on forgiving him.'

✠

Saint Stephen even forgave the people who were killing him.

The Reading comes from the Story of the Apostles.

One day, the twelve apostles
called a meeting of the friends of Jesus, and said:
We need someone to help us
to give out food
and look after people,
then *we* can teach and pray.

So they picked out Philip and Stephen and five others.
Then they prayed for them
and they blessed them,
　stretching their hands over them.

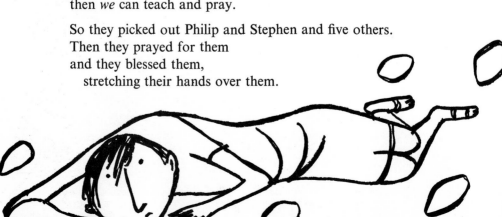

Stephen did wonderful things,
for he was very clever,
and the Holy Spirit helped him.
But some people told lies about him
    and had him arrested and put in prison.

The judge asked Stephen questions,
but no one would listen to his answers.
They put their hands over their ears,
    so they couldn't hear what he was saying.
Then they pulled him to a place outside the city
    and they threw stones at him
        until they killed him.

But before he died, Stephen said,
'Lord Jesus, I give you my life!
Do not blame them for doing wrong!'

✠ SAINT PHILIP AND THE MAN IN A CHARIOT

Jesus and 'The Twelve' baptised many people.

The Reading comes from the Gospel of Saint John.

Jesus went with his friends into the countryside of Judea,
and he stayed there
   baptising many people
   – or at least his friends did.
They baptised even more people than John the Baptist.

But the Pharisees heard about it
   and they didn't like it.
So Jesus left Judea
and went back to Galilee.

✠

Saint Philip teaches a foreigner about Jesus and baptises him.

The Reading comes from the Story of the Apostles.

One of the followers of Jesus was called Philip.
One day Philip went out for a walk
along the desert road near Jerusalem.

As he was walking,
an important man went past in a chariot.
He was from Ethiopia
and was on his way home

As he went along
he was reading the Bible
and Philip said,
'Do you understand what you are reading?'
'How can I by myself?' said the man,
'Come up here and sit beside me
   and explain it all.'

So Philip did,
and he went on to explain what Jesus had done.

After a while they came to some water,
and the man said,
'Is there any reason why I shouldn't be baptised here and now?'
and Philip said, 'No.'
So they stopped the chariot and got down,
and Philip baptised the man at once.

41

✠ A PRIEST CALLED 'JOSEPH BARNABAS'

Jesus said, 'I want you to tell everyone what I have told you.'
The Reading comes from the Gospel of Saint Mark.

One day, Jesus said to his friends:

'Go out to the whole world.
Tell everyone what I have done
and baptise everyone who believes what you say.'

And they did just that:
after Jesus had died,
they talked about him everywhere.
And even though they could not see him,
Jesus helped them all the time.

✠

Joseph Barnabas made the followers of Christ so well known that they
were called 'Christ-ians' by everyone else.

The Reading comes from the Story of the Apostles.

One of the followers of Jesus
was a priest called Joseph Barnabas.
This man owned a field,
but he sold it
and gave the money he got for it to 'The Twelve'.

Later on
when Paul became a follower of Jesus
and everyone was afraid of him,
because they thought he was just pretending,
Joseph Barnabas took Paul to 'The Twelve'
and told them Paul's story,
so that people would trust Paul,
(even though he *had* been their enemy!)

Barnabas was a good man,
and the Holy Spirit filled him with the love of God.
So 'The Twelve' sent him to Antioch
   to help the followers of Jesus there.
And he taught a lot of people to know and love Jesus.

Then he went off to find Paul again,
and he brought Paul back to Antioch.
They stayed there together for twelve months,
teaching everyone about Jesus.
This made the followers of Jesus Christ so well known
that they were called 'the Christ-ians'
because they followed 'Christ'.

✠ EVERYONE IS WELCOME IN THE PEOPLE OF GOD!

God the Father wants people to come and be happy with him. Some people don't seem to be interested – they just can't be bothered to follow his Son, Jesus. So God invites other people – in fact he invites everyone! He doesn't want anyone to be left out!

The Reading comes from the Gospel of St Luke.

One day Jesus told this story.

There was once a man who gave a great banquet
and invited many people to it.
When everything was ready,
he sent out his son to tell the guests
   to come and join him.
But each one of them began to make excuses.

One of the guests said,
'I've just bought a field,
and I have to go and look at it.
I'm sorry. I cannot come.'

Another guest said,
'I've just bought five pair of oxen,
and I've got to go and see what they're like.
I'm sorry. I cannot come.'
Yet another guest said,
'What a pity. I've just been married.
I'm sorry. I cannot come.'

When the man heard all this, he was furious,
and he said to his son,
'These people don't *deserve* to enjoy my banquet!
Go out into the streets and the alley-ways of the town,
and bring in the poor, the crippled, the blind and the lame.
Bring *them* into my banquet instead!'

When this was done, there was still some more room left,
and so the man said,
'Go right out into the country roads and lanes
and *make* people come in.
I don't want my house to be empty for the banquet!
I want it to be absolutely full!'

✪ YOU ARE THE LUCKY PEOPLE!

Jesus sometimes said things in a strange way.
He obviously wanted people to puzzle out what he meant.
He wanted to make them 'think'.
Here are some of the most famous of these puzzling 'riddles' that Jesus used.

The Reading comes from the Gospel of Saint Matthew.

Jesus said these things to his friends.

'How lucky you are, if you are poor!
God will make you rich!'

'How lucky you are, if you are not very important!
God will make you great!'

'How lucky you are, if you are keen to do what *God* wants!
God will see that you get what *you* want as well!'

'How lucky you are, if you forgive others!
God will forgive you!'

'How lucky you are if you really want to know God!
God will make sure you get to know him well!'

'How lucky you are, if you help people to be friends!
God will be friends with you!'

'How lucky you are, if people attack you,
   especially when you are trying to do what God wants!
God will welcome you with open arms!'